Introduction:

This booklet contains a full practice e
with the practice experience needed to
This practice exam should help you see whether you have not only
memorized your study material, but are also able to apply it, which
is the only way to pass the exam.

There are 90 questions, distributed over 18 cases. The score to aim
for is 80% correct, meaning 18 mistakes or fewer. If you scored
80% or higher, consider yourself ready for exam day.

How to take this practice exam:

Take a piece of paper, a pencil, and a timer. Set the timer for 2.5
hours. Write down the number of the question and the answer you
think is correct. If you do not immediately know the correct
answer, or you would like to review your answer at the end, write a
question mark behind that question. This indicates that you flagged
the answer for later review, so you do not waste time if you are
stuck (very useful during the actual exam as well!).

Afterward, go to the answer section of this booklet. The answer
key is provided, which allows you to determine your score. An
explanation is provided in the last section of this booklet. Keep in
mind that it is important to understand the logic behind the
questions and answers, since that is one of the benefits of using
this practice exam.

About this document:

The practice exams currently available are incomplete, expensive, and treacherously easy. This practice exam provides you with more of a challenge than the alternatives. The brief explanations should help you understand the way questions can be phrased and how to choose the best answer.

After using this booklet as intended, combined with your regular study material, you should have improved your speed and accuracy, leaving you with sufficient time to go back to review the questions you flagged.

The topics and types of questions in this practice exam are balanced to resemble the actual exam. However, if you would like to test your skills in applying the privacy laws from your study material further than this practice exam, please try "Full CIPP/US Practice Exam - Case Study Edition", which contains material to focus specifically on the scenario questions part (which will be the most difficult part of the exam) and provides more of a challenge to test whether you really understand the material.

Good luck!

Kind regards,

Jasper Jacobs, CIPP/E, CIPP/US, CIPM, CIPT

EXAM QUESTIONS:

1. Which branch of government generally has the final say in the passing of a law?

A. the executive branch

B. the legislative branch

C. the operational branch

D. the judicial branch

2. Which branch of government does the president belong to?

A. the judicial branch

B. the executive branch

C. the operational branch

D. none of these answers

3. How can personal information best be described?

A. any information relating to a natural person

B. this depends on the field and even state law

C. directory information

D. information of value

4. Which comprehensive federal privacy laws are there in the US?

A. the Children's Online Privacy Protection Act

B. the Health Insurance Portability and Accountability Act

C. none, there are no comprehensive federal privacy laws in the US

D. the General Data Protection Regulation

5. Of the following, which are three different tort categories?

A. negligence, notice breach, intrusion

B. intrusion upon seclusion, strict liability, negligence with blame

C. intentional, negligent, strict liability

D. privacy notice breach, wrongful intrusion, defamation

6. What is the best description of the difference between criminal and civil liability?

A. civil cases are the only cases with victims

B. criminal cases involve entities and persons

C. civil cases are between persons and/or entities, whereas criminal cases are brought by the government

D. in a civil case no laws are broken

7. In relation to privacy, which of the following is most restrictive for employers in the US?

A. the Health Insurance Portability and Accountability Act

B. the Children's Online Privacy Protection Act

C. the Fourth Amendment

D. the Fair and Accurate Credit Transactions Act

8. What is the most likely purpose for which an organization creates a data inventory?

A. showing the public which data are stored

B. creating an overview of data, helpful for creating a compliance and security approach

C. complying with a US legal requirement

D. identifying storage size requirements

9. Which of the following statements is not true regarding data classification?

A. organizations are free to classify data elements a certain way to place it inside or outside the scope of certain laws

B. data classification can help identify applicable laws

C. to assist in creating a security strategy

D. help breach response

Use this scenario for the following three questions:

A tech startup in San Francisco developed software that analyzes the movements of athletes, both for generating feedback to improve posture and for movement effectiveness. With the results of the software analyses, the athlete's performance and health should improve.

The startup has performed hundreds of analyses to test its software, the results of which are all stored on a server in San Diego. Of the hundreds of analyses, half of them have been performed on publicly broadcasted sports games, from every continent.

To sell the software, potential customers are provided with a 30-day trial, as well as the results of all analyses of public broadcasts. Especially the public broadcasts are a conversation starter amongst those who have access, because everyone loves criticizing successful athletes for some reason.

Then, on a dark and rainy night, a disgruntled ex-employee releases all test analyses and customer information publicly. The leak is all over the news, and copies of the analyses rapidly spread through peer-to-peer sharing networks.

10. Which of the following laws would you advise the startup to look at first?

A. the Health Insurance Portability and Accountability Act

B. the Sports Data Analysis Act

C. the constitution

D. California SB 1386

11. Besides causing a breach in the US, will there be foreign legislation applicable?

A. the General Data Protection Regulation is applicable, because matches from Europe have been analyzed

B. the matches used from outside the US were publicly available, so there are no responsibilities

C. the matches used from outside the US were publicly available, so there are no liabilities

D. if the data protection authorities are notified timely, there will be no adverse effects

12. What is the most likely course of action by the startup?

A. change the encryption software

B. tell their customers what happened

C. do nothing, as there was no security breach since the ex-employee logged in with his password to remove the encryption

D. update their privacy notice to reflect current practices

13. What is not the result of an organization starting a privacy program?

A. awareness amongst employees

B. reduced risk of compliance issues

C. an improvement of the breach detection rate and breach response time

D. full future-proof compliance with privacy legislation

14. Which of the following contains specific data retention and disposal requirements?

A. the Fair and Accurate Credit Transactions Act

B. any pre-emptive law

C. the Children's Online Privacy Protection Act

D. the Cable Communications Policy Act

15. Which of the following is not applicable to international data transfers?

A. the Fair and Accurate Credit Transactions Act

B. the General Data Protection Regulation

C. the CLOUD Act

D. the Personal Information Protection and Electronic Documents Act

16. How can security in relation to privacy be described best?

A. privacy deserves higher priority than security

B. privacy needs security, but security is not only about privacy

C. security and privacy have no overlap

D. de-identified data do not require security measures

17. Which of the following is not an appropriate way for an international organization operating in the US to be compliant with European Privacy regulations?

A. standard contractual clauses

B. European ownership of the organization

C. Binding Corporate Rules

D. keeping all data in the country of origin

18. Which of the following is true about privacy notices?

A. only certain US laws require a privacy notice

B. privacy notices are required for all websites in the US or targeted at a US audience

C. changing a privacy notice mid-service is not deceptive

D. the CLOUD Act

19. What does workforce training on privacy matters establish?

A. it eliminates all compliance risk

B. the training motivates the workforce, and allows the workforce to work more efficiently

C. it shows that management delegates the process of becoming compliant

D. increase the level of knowledge of staff, decreasing the chance of non-compliance

20. A merger between a US based company, and affiliates in Asia and Canada is planned to take place. As a privacy officer, what considerations would you bring to the CEO's attention?

A. Canada's non-Personal Information Protection and Electronic Documents Act legislation

B. the potential benefits of sharing data

C. an expansion of your department and an increase in salary

D. data flow mapping

21. What is one of the important considerations for companies selling to consumers internationally?

A. the salary of the privacy officers

B. whether they actively target customers in other countries

C. Bring Your Own Device practices

D. the Fourth amendment

22. What is the name of the guidelines developed by the Asia-Pacific Economic Cooperation?

A. the OECD guidelines

B. the IT Act

C. the Fair Information Practices

D. the APEC privacy framework

23. Which of the following is not a key attribute of security?

A. Confidentiality

B. Delivery

C. Integrity

D. Availability

24. Which types of security controls can be considered in developing a security strategy?

A. physical, administrative, technical

B. proactive, reactive, distortive

C. detective, cumulative reactive

D. physical, cosmetic, digital

25. What is the best fitting description of a data breach?

A. a failure of security measures, resulting in the unauthorized accessing of data

B. loss of data, including an encrypted hard drive

C. a shutdown of the company server

D. the National Security Agency has access to classified information

26. After a data breach, there are several ways to deal with the breach. Which of the following is the least likely reason for correctly dealing with incidents?

A. to comply with legislation

B. to minimize adverse consequences

C. to hide security flaws

D. to fix any security weaknesses

27. What is the biggest reason online privacy is a complicated thing?

A. smart devices automatically gather data

B. the Internet of Things is not controllable

C. people are social media addicts, and unable to stop sharing personal information

D. it is decentralized, non-transparent with a large collection of (seemingly) restrictive and contradicting legislation

28. When a consent decree is published, what has happened?

A. a lawsuit is started regarding a data breach, resulting in a publication of the appropriate security policy

B. the Federal Trade Commission and the other party entered into an agreement to stop a certain conduct, and the information is published for other organizations to learn from

C. compensation is paid to the victims, so they cannot start a lawsuit

D. Binding Corporate Rules are implemented, ensuring consistent practices across all affiliates

29. How can the Federal Trade Commission be described best?

A. a part of the executive branch with rule-making powers

B. a counterpart of the European Parliament

C. the enforcer of the Fourth amendment

D. the Federal Trade Commission has won every case

Use this scenario for the following two questions:

A well-known social media website called *Selfie Shenanigans* is constantly innovating. Innovating, of course, means finding ways to make a product out of its users. Users are incredibly happy with all services the website provides, and the website is working hard to keep figuring out new functionalities that users did not yet know they need.

In the next month, Selfie Shenanigans is planning to implement its newest feature in the US, only for its US users. The new feature allows Selfie Shenanigans to analyze all uploaded photos for visible signs of health issues, thus potentially algorithmically making life saving medical diagnoses.

Building a website is not cheap, and the CEO has so little money that he is basically an altruistic volunteer, so the data are sold to the user's health insurance company so it can inform the user of his or her medical diagnosis, if the health insurance company's records show that the user has not already received the required treatment.

You have been hired as a legal consultant, with the message that "the feature is getting implemented no matter what, but we just need you to tell us how to prevent trouble". The message is clear, and how you feel morally is not of importance.

30. Which law would least possibly be broken?

A. the Health Insurance Portability and Accountability Act

B. the Children's Online Privacy Protection Act

C. the General Data Protection Regulation

D. the Health Information Technology for Economic and Clinical Health Act

31. You find out that the website has a privacy notice that is shown before users sign up. What needs to happen?

A. the privacy notice needs to be changed, ensuring that the new feature can be implemented

B. a check whether the new practice is allowed for, according to the privacy notice, needs to be performed

C. all children under 13 years of age need to sign a new privacy notice

D. nothing, there is a privacy notice already, so it is fine, no need to worry

32. When does the Children's Online Privacy Protection Act apply?

A. for websites targeting children under 18

B. for websites targeting children under 13

C. for websites without a privacy notice

D. for websites that store de-identified data of toddlers

33. For which law does the Federal Trade Commission have specific authority?

A. the General Data Protection Regulation

B. the Children's Online Privacy Protection Act

C. the APEC Privacy Framework

D. the Fair Information Practices

34. There are several laws concerning medical privacy, both on national and state level. Which of the following is the most likely reason for this legislation?

A. medical data are in high demand, hence legislation is needed to guide medical practitioners in the selling of such data

B. privacy is an absolute right, and therefore requires protection

C. organ theft is a major issue, and unsafely stored medical records were a valuable source of information for organ thieves

D. it is believed that patients are more open and honest about their conditions if they experience a sense of privacy

35. What safeguard is often put in place by researchers when using medical data for research?

A. non-disclosure agreement

B. encryption of data

C. the data is de-identified

D. patient consent form

36. The Health Insurance Portability and Accountability Act is quite strict. Which of the following statements is most accurate?

A. all medical data are covered by the Health Insurance Portability and Accountability Act

B. the Health Insurance Portability and Accountability Act is based on the Fifth amendment

C. aspects of the Health Insurance Portability and Accountability Act can be disregarded when stricter state law is in place

D. all medical practitioners sign a Health Insurance Portability and Accountability Act declaration before being authorized to practice medicine

37. Which of the following best describes the privacy rights of a person visiting a doctor?

A. an absolute right, with full control over every aspect of the data, including control over the use for research

B. covered by the Health Insurance Portability and Accountability Act for the electronic transactions for the treatment, as well as the Reader Privacy Act for the book he bought in California to learn about the disease

C. the medical data derived from the visit to the doctor can under no circumstances be used for research

D. only the government is forbidden access to the data, based on the Fourth amendment, which includes e-health data generated by medical practitioners

38. According to the Confidentiality of Substance Use Disorder Patient Record Rule, what is required for disclosure of patient information?

A. a recommendation from the patient's counselor

B. fully documented parental consent, regardless of the age of the patient

C. written patient consent, explicitly describing the type of information to be disclosed

D. under no circumstances is patient information to be disclosed

39. What was the initial reason for the Health Insurance Portability and Accountability Act?

A. patient privacy and security

B. to define Personal Health Information

C. to define electronic Personal Health Information

D. the improvement of the efficiency of delivery of health care

40. What is one of the limitations of the Health Insurance Portability and Accountability Act?

A. the Health Information Technology for Economic and Clinical Health Act was needed to define electronic Personal Health Information

B. the Health Insurance Portability and Accountability Act is a guideline and not a law

C. the Health Insurance Portability and Accountability Act is not applicable to situations involving retired citizens

D. some doctors are not covered by the Health Insurance Portability and Accountability Act

41. Which of the following is not a key privacy protection under the Health Insurance Portability and Accountability Act?

A. layered privacy notices

B. administrative, physical and technical safeguards

C. a privacy professional for covered entities

D. individuals are allowed to access and copy a designated record set

42. Which of the following preempts state law in most areas?

A. the Fair and Accurate Credit Transactions Act

B. the Fair Credit Reporting Act

C. the Gramm-Leach-Bliley Act

D. the Financial Turmoil Reconciliation Assurance Act

43. The Fair Credit Reporting Act affects organizations like Equifax, Experian and TransUnion. What are these organizations classified as?

A. Consumer Reporting Agencies

B. Credit Reporting Agencies

C. Credit Score Agencies

D. Transaction Recording Agencies

44. Which of the following is required by the Fair and Accurate Credit Transactions Act and enhances privacy?

A. receipts are legally stored for a period of seven years

B. credit card numbers are only allowed to be stored without the accompanying signature

C. receipts are not allowed to reveal a full credit card number or debit card number

D. receipts are only allowed to be issued digitally in specific situations

45. How can the disposal rule be most accurately described?

A. making sure unauthorized recipients dispose of a consumer report after there is no legal basis for it anymore

B. when issued, the unnecessary information is disposed of before issuing a report

C. physical copies need to be scanned and disposed of, and digital storage needs to be encrypted

D. a way to ensure that a consumer report is disposed of properly after it is no longer needed or allowed to be used

46. Which of the following is not true regarding the Red Flag Rule?

A. originally required through the Fair and Accurate Credit Transactions Act

B. authorized the Federal Trade Commission & federal banking agencies

C. certain financial entities are required to develop an identity theft detection program

D. requires insurance against Identity Theft

47. What was U.S. Bancorp accused of?

A. not properly encrypting the credit card data of its customers

B. illegal data transfers to India, due to outsourcing

C. sharing detailed customer information with a telemarketing firm

D. storing data of minors without the required parental consent

48. What kind of institutions fall within the scope of the Family Educational Rights and Privacy Act?

A. all educational institutions fall within the scope

B. educational institutions that receive federal funding

C. it applies to educational institutions with exchange students

D. privately funded educational institutions

49. Which type of information is still allowed to be disclosed under the Family Educational Rights and Privacy Act?

A. Grade Point Average

B. directory information

C. home addresses of students

D. health insurance coverage

50. Which of the following best describes the US National Do Not Call Registry?

A. a program implemented by the Federal Communications Commission, where phone numbers of US residents can be registered to be placed in the registry

B. the requirement for citizens to actively indicate that they are open to receiving unsolicited phone calls

C. a program implemented by the Federal Trade Commission, where phone numbers can be registered to be placed in the registry

D. an initiative that was sparked by the concept of the Internet of Things

51. What is not true about the Do Not Call Registry?

A. sellers and telemarketers are required to update their call lists annually

B. only sellers, telemarketers, and service providers may access the registry

C. violations can lead to civil penalties

D. the Do Not Call Registry is implemented by the Federal Trade Commission

52. Which of the following is not true regarding consent to allow telemarketers and sellers to call a consumer?

A. must include a signature

B. consent requires a privacy notice

C. must be in writing

D. consent must be clear and conspicuous

53. What are robocalls?

A. phone calls established through the automated dialing of random numbers

B. phone calls augmented with Artificial Intelligence

C. communication established through the Internet of Things

D. prerecorded calls

54. The goal of the Controlling the Assault of Non-Solicited Pornography And Marketing Act is best described as which of the following?

A. apply a paternalistic filtering of pornographic material so as to raise slipping moral standards

B. a way to respect individual rights and provide a way to indicate how desirable the communication is

C. eliminate phishing attacks, and reducing the financial burden it causes

D. allow parents to be in control over what messages their children receive

55. Which of the following can be said about the Cable Communications Policy Act?

A. video rental records cannot be disclosed freely

B. it has become redundant due to internet television

C. certain damages as a result of violations can be recovered because it provides for private right of action

D. there is no such law as the Cable Communications Policy Act

56. Which state was the first to include a Do Not Track requirement in its laws?

A. New York

B. California

C. Washington

D. North Carolina

57. Due to the 2007 revisions to the Federal Rules of Civil Procedure, what is now required?

A. a non-disclosure requirement for members of the jury

B. names omitted in court cases

C. encryption of e-discovery data

D. redacting sensitive personal information

58. Which of the following is not required for a subpoena according to the Federal Rule of Civil Procedure 45?

A. state the court from which it is issued

B. state the title of the action and its civil action number

C. take photographic evidence of the receipt of the subpoena

D. mention a person's right to challenge or modify the subpoena

59. How can courts prohibit the disclosure of personal information used or generated in litigation?

A. the court can issue a protective order

B. the court can issue a restrictive order

C. the court can issue a redactive order

D. the court can issue a national security letter

60. What was the main concern when posting personal information used in bankruptcy cases online?

A. stalking

B. family feuds

C. identity theft

D. data breaches

61. Which of the following is not one of the four key guidelines from the Sedona Conference?

A. professionals from several disciplines should provide input into the e-mail retention policy

B. e-mail retention policies should continually be developed

C. a Chief Information Security Officer in charge of e-discovery

D. industry standards should be taken into account

62. What is the Communications Assistance to Law Enforcement Act also referred to?

A. the Pen Register

B. the Digital Telephony Bill

C. the Wire

D. Track and Trace

63. In 2016 the FBI was quarrelling with Apple. What was the quarrel about?

A. new firmware slowing down phones

B. helping gain access to the data on a seized phone

C. the tablets in the Federal Bureau of Investigation's office could not fit the micro-SD required for the investigation

D. a cloud security breach exposing pictures of celebrities

64. Which of the following is most accurate regarding workplace privacy?

A. workplace privacy is the same in every state

B. US privacy protection at the workplace is the strictest in the world

C. workers have a high level of influence in workplace practices

D. there is no law that covers privacy specifically

65. Which of the following is not a source of privacy protection for employees?

A. state labor laws

B. contract and tort law

C. overarching employment privacy law

D. certain federal laws

66. What is the most accurate comparison between US and EU workplace privacy?

A. the US inspired the EU legislation

B. the EU has no law that is applicable to the workplace

C. the US has cubicles, whereas in the EU cubicles are forbidden because of privacy concerns

D. EU employee data fall under the scope of the General Data Protection Regulation and offers more protection than all US laws combined

67. What can be said about the Constitution's Fourth Amendment?

A. it provides protection from employers

B. it provides protection from government employers

C. it does not concern privacy

D. it only protects against the king of England

68. In the US, there is employment at will. What is a consequence of this?

A. all legislation is rendered invalid

B. you can buy privacy

C. many aspects, covered by laws in other continents, are at the discretion of the employer

D. employees have no rights

69. Which of the following is not a tort that can be relied on by an employee in a privacy case?

A. intrusion upon seclusion

B. publicity given to private life

C. defamation

D. intellectual property

70. Of the following laws, which does not have employment privacy implications?

A. the Children's Online Privacy Protection Act

B. the Employee Retirement Income Security Act

C. the Health Insurance Portability and Accountability Act

D. the Fair Labor Standards Act

71. At which state of employment do employers need to take into account workplace privacy considerations?

A. before employment

B. before, during, and after employment

C. during employment

D. after employment

72. What is true about Bring Your Own Device policies?

A. only company-issued equipment is allowed to be used

B. it brings along security risks and requires reconsideration of the level of monitoring

C. employees surrender their data when a Bring Your Own Device policy is in place

D. Bring Your Own Device practices are illegal

73. Which of the following is a consequence of the Employee Polygraph Protection Act?

A. only grade A and B type polygraphs are allowed to be used

B. an employer cannot use a polygraph test to screen an applicant

C. a statement of sincerity is required to substitute a polygraph

D. employers cannot screen applicants

74. Which of the following agencies is not responsible for privacy enforcement?

A. the Federal Trade Commission

B. the Department of Education

C. the Federal Communications Commission

D. certain agencies part of the executive branch

75. What is true for the Federal Trade Commission?

A. the Federal Trade Commission is an independent agency

B. the Federal Trade Commission falls under direct control of the president

C. the Federal Trade Commission focuses solely on privacy

D. the Federal Trade Commission focuses solely on security

76. What was the issue in the Designerware, LLC case?

A. the leaking of credit card numbers

B. key loggers, unexpected screenshots and photographs

C. a break-in on one of the servers that stored social security numbers

D. unauthorized disclosure of collected sensitive data

77. When is a data breach required to be reported?

A. above 200 persons

B. above 100 persons

C. if minors are involved

D. depends on the state and breach size

78. Is ransomware a data breach?

A. always

B. never

C. depends on whether unauthorized access has been established

D. not if the information was backed up

Use this scenario for the following four questions:

A US-based supermarket chain called *Vallmart* performed poorly the last few months, due to a scandal which involved one of its employees dying because of exhaustion after a 20-hour shift. Vallmart executives tried to restore the store's reputation by offering all employees free in-house medical checkups. To keep things fair for those employees who already underwent a medical checkup at their regular doctor, Vallmart will reimburse any checkups already performed (up to a certain amount, of course).

As a second move to improve revenue, an aggressive takeover of the French Parrefour has taken place. Parrefour has an excellent customer loyalty program, which Vallmart is planning to merge with its own customer loyalty program. Doing so will allow Vallmart to predict global trends based on the data collected through the loyalty cards.

You are the Chief Privacy Officer of Vallmart, in charge of both the privacy officers of Vallmart and the privacy officers of the recently acquired Parrefour. Although you are not trained in European privacy law, you are aware of the potential existence of differences.

79. From an organizational perspective, what is likely the most prudent course of action?

A. place the US team in charge of the US data

B. request the US-based and EU-based privacy officers to educate each other on the applicable laws in their continent

C. place the EU team in charge of the EU data

D. fire the EU team and train the US team on EU law

80. What is the most likely scenario for the use of the EU customer data?

A. the company is under full US ownership, so the data can be used freely

B. the data of the EU customers are deleted

C. the data cannot be used until the required safeguards are put in place

D. All EU customers receive a notice and a one-off discount on their shopping, agreeing their data are used in the US

81. Now that the US-based Vallmart has complete ownership of Parrefour, which of the following is most likely true?

A. US data are forbidden to be processed in Europe

B. the Federal Trade Commission and the Federal Communications Commission are the regulatory authorities that Vallmart has to answer to

C. US customers are granted the same rights in the US as Europeans had in Europe

D. medical information of US employees is free to be stored in Europe without additional safeguards

82. Which of the following is most probable regarding workplace monitoring at Vallmart (including Parrefour)?

A. the company is US owned now, so either accept it or find a new job (employment at will)

B. the US practices may have to be revised

C. a salary increase for EU employees will be negotiated with the labor unions to compensate for the loss of privacy

D. Europe is full of socialists, so the workers will not mind sacrificing privacy for the greater good (the company)

83. Certain national laws preempt state law. Out of the following choices, how can preempting best be described?

A. a privacy notice, under many circumstances, can be overruled by state law

B. laws of an inferior government can be superseded by those of a superior government

C. if a state has no law, it is preempted by national law

D. federal judges can preempt the president and a large part of the executive branch

84. Although there are many actions an individual can take to battle injustice, which of the following most accurately describes private right of action?

A. to carry a concealed weapon and use it to protect your privacy when someone attempts to enter your domicile

B. to start a lawsuit when a law is violated

C. to enforce the binding rules of a privacy notice

D. to forbid organizations from processing the data of minors that you are the legal guardian of

85. If an agency has authority, there are two types of authority that agency can have. Which type of authority does the Federal Trade Commission have?

A. general authority

B. specific authority

C. general authority as well as specific authority

D. operational authority

86. Many references to privacy can be found all throughout recorded history. When looking at laws regarding personal information, which class of privacy does law concerning personal information pertain to?

A. bodily privacy

B. territorial privacy

C. communications privacy

D. information privacy

87. Which of the following is not (yet) part of the Fair Information Practices?

A. notice

B. choice and consent

C. disclosure

D. legal basis

88. All over the world, different models of privacy protection are adopted. Which of the following is true regarding models of privacy protection?

A. in the US there is a sectoral model, and in the EU there is a comprehensive model

B. the US only uses the co-regulatory model

C. Europe has a strong focus on the self-regulatory model

D. the laws in the US fall under the comprehensive model

89. Which of the following best describes the relationship between case law and common law?

A. common law needs case law to exist

B. common law is based on principles

C. case law is solely the judge's opinion

D. case law is fluid, and allows for presidential intervention

90. When can an organization most likely be in trouble for violating contract law?

A. when someone provided his or her data based on the practices mentioned in the privacy notice

B. when a data subject disagrees with a privacy notice

C. when a privacy notice is not in the local language

D. when a privacy notice is not on the organization's website

CORRECT ANSWERS:

1B	24A	47C	70A
2B	25A	48B	71B
3B	26C	49B	72B
4C	27D	50C	73B
5C	28B	51A	74B
6C	29A	52B	75A
7C	30C	53D	76B
8B	31B	54B	77D
9A	32B	55C	78C
10D	33B	56B	79B
11A	34D	57D	80C
12B	35C	58C	81B
13D	36C	59A	82B
14A	37B	60C	83B
15A	38C	61C	84B
16B	39D	62B	85C
17B	40D	63B	86D
18A	41A	64D	87D
19D	42A	65C	88A
20D	43A	66D	89A
21B	44C	67B	90A
22D	45D	68C	
23B	46D	69D	

QUESTIONS WITH BRIEF EXPLANATIONS:

1. Which branch of government generally has the final say in the passing of a law?

A. the executive branch

B. the legislative branch (correct)

C. the operational branch

D. the judicial branch

Explanation: the legislate branch (congress) votes on the passing of a law. The president can veto, but then congress can still vote for the bill to become a law, hence B is the correct answer. Do not spend your study time on exceptions such as pocket vetoes, unless they are specifically highlighted in your study materials.

2. Which branch of government does the president belong to?

A. the judicial branch

B. the executive branch (correct)

C. the operational branch

D. none of these answers

Explanation: the president is part of the executive branch, hence B is the correct answer.

3. How can personal information best be described?

A. any information relating to a natural person

B. this depends on the field and even state law (correct)

C. directory information

D. information of value

Explanation: there are laws for different disciplines/fields/areas, which can also differ per state. The most correct answer is B, since the point here is that there is no clear definition. A would be the correct answer in Europe, and with all the attention the legislation there is getting this is not a bad definition to remember. C is a label and not a description, and D is nonsense.

4. Which comprehensive federal privacy laws are there in the US?

A. the Children's Online Privacy Protection Act

B. the Health Insurance Portability and Accountability Act

C. none, there are no comprehensive federal privacy laws in the US (correct)

D. the General Data Protection Regulation

Explanation: no single law covers privacy comprehensively, and US privacy legislation is mostly sectoral. Hence C is the correct answer. A and B are laws but not comprehensive. D could be argued to be correct as well since it can also apply in the US, but it is not a US law so not the answer here.

5. Of the following, which are three different tort categories?

A. negligence, notice breach, intrusion

B. intrusion upon seclusion, strict liability, negligence with blame

C. intentional, negligent, strict liability (correct)

D. privacy notice breach, wrongful intrusion, defamation

Explanation: A, B and D contain several non-torts, so C is the correct answer.

6. What is the best description of the difference between criminal and civil liability?

A. civil cases are the only cases with victims

B. criminal cases involve entities and persons

C. civil cases are between persons and/or entities, whereas criminal cases are brought by the government (correct)

D. in a civil case no laws are broken

Explanation: C is the only correct answer, the others have false parts in them. Regardless of the false parts, option C is the only answer that contrasts civil and criminal, which is what was asked for. Be aware of what is asked, since it is easy to focus on the wrong thing.

7. In relation to privacy, which of the following is most restrictive for employers in the US?

A. the Health Insurance Portability and Accountability Act

B. the Children's Online Privacy Protection Act

C. the Fourth Amendment (correct)

D. the Fair and Accurate Credit Transactions Act

Explanation: the Fourth Amendment is applicable to government searches, hence applies to how governmental employers treat their employees. A could also have implications, especially when a company provides health care, but the Fourth Amendment has a clear link.

8. What is the most likely purpose for which an organization creates a data inventory?

A. showing the public which data are stored

B. creating an overview of data, helpful for creating a compliance and security approach (correct)

C. complying with a US legal requirement

D. identifying storage size requirements

Explanation: A is nonsense, C is true in Europe but not (yet) in the US, D could be true but storage requirements should also be obvious without a data inventory, hence B remains. When you create a data inventory, you know what type of personal information you have and for what reason, which you can use to see how you want to protect it and which laws apply.

9. Which of the following statements is not true regarding data classification?

A. organizations are free to classify data elements a certain way to place it inside or outside the scope of certain laws (correct)

B. data classification can help identify applicable laws

C. to assist in creating a security strategy

D. help breach response

Explanation: B, C and D are true. A is not true, because if it were true that would be scary since classifying data a certain way does not change the actual data (and the risks that having these data brings along).

Use this scenario for the following three questions:

A tech startup in San Francisco developed software that analyzes the movements of athletes, both for generating feedback to improve posture and for movement effectiveness. With the results of the software analyses, the athlete's performance and health should improve.

The startup has performed hundreds of analyses to test its software, the results of which are all stored on a server in San Diego. Of the hundreds of analyses, half of them have been performed on publicly broadcasted sports games, from every continent.

To sell the software, potential customers are provided with a 30-day trial, as well as the results of all analyses of public broadcasts. Especially the public broadcasts are a conversation starter amongst those who have access, because everyone loves criticizing successful athletes for some reason.

Then, on a dark and rainy night, a disgruntled ex-employee releases all test analyses and customer information publicly. The leak is all over the news, and copies of the analyses rapidly spread through peer-to-peer sharing networks.

10. Which of the following laws would you advise the startup to look at first?

A. the Health Insurance Portability and Accountability Act

B. the Sports Data Analysis Act

C. the constitution

D. California SB 1386 (correct)

Explanation: since the company is in California, and a big leak just occurred, the law that addresses breaches (California SB 1386) would be useful to check to see if any actions are required and whether the events constitute a breach. So, D is the correct answer.

11. Besides causing a breach in the US, will there be foreign legislation applicable?

A. the General Data Protection Regulation is applicable, because matches from Europe have been analyzed (correct)

B. the matches used from outside the US were publicly available, so there are no responsibilities

C. the matches used from outside the US were publicly available, so there are no liabilities

D. if the data protection authorities are notified timely, there will be no adverse effects

Explanation: as a US privacy professional, it will not hurt to be aware of the legislation in other continents. In Europe a lot is happening right now, and in other continents are following. And, since the GDPR applies to all personal data of EU citizens, whether processed inside or outside of the EU, the GDPR applies and A is the correct answer. Also, it is important to be aware that not only the public data that were leaked, but also the newly generated data (the analyses).

12. What is the most likely course of action by the startup?

A. change the encryption software

B. tell their customers what happened (correct)

C. do nothing, as there was no security breach since the ex-employee logged in with his password to remove the encryption

D. update their privacy notice to reflect current practices

Explanation: the most likely course of action is to inform the customers so they can take action if needed. This would be more important if the information were more sensitive, but B is still the correct answer. A is not needed since the encryption was not broken, C does not do justice to the victims and D does not remedy what happened.

13. What is not the result of an organization starting a privacy program?

A. awareness amongst employees

B. reduced risk of compliance issues

C. an improvement of the breach detection rate and breach response time

D. full future-proof compliance with privacy legislation (correct)

Explanation: you can aim for compliance with a privacy program, and it will have some effect, but there cannot be any guarantees for future compliance with changing legislation. Hence, D is the correct answer.

14. Which of the following contains specific data retention and disposal requirements?

A. the Fair and Accurate Credit Transactions Act (correct)

B. any pre-emptive law

C. the Children's Online Privacy Protection Act

D. the Cable Communications Policy Act

Explanation: just a fact, A is the correct answer. Also important to remember, is that FACTA preempts state law.

15. Which of the following is not applicable to international data transfers?

A. the Fair and Accurate Credit Transactions Act (correct)

B. the General Data Protection Regulation

C. the CLOUD Act

D. the Personal Information Protection and Electronic Documents Act

Explanation: FACTA is least likely to have international consequences (although there might be small exceptions), so A is the correct answer. B is the European law that definitely is applicable, as is C because it concerns accessing data stored abroad. D is the Canadian law that is relatively comprehensive, and also applies to data being sent abroad. The answer here is tricky, but eliminating the obvious wrong choices leads to the most correct answer.

16. How can security in relation to privacy be described best?

A. privacy deserves higher priority than security

B. privacy needs security, but security is not only about privacy (correct)

C. security and privacy have no overlap

D. de-identified data do not require security measures

Explanation: this is a vague question, which was the intention. A is subjective and could be true, but since B is objective and true it is the correct answer. Handling personal information requires a certain level of security, so privacy needs security. Security is also needed for non-personal information, so it is not only about privacy. C is just wrong, and D as well since you may have a valuable de-identified data set that you want to protect from others.

17. Which of the following is not an appropriate way for an international organization operating in the US to be compliant with European Privacy regulations?

A. standard contractual clauses

B. European ownership of the organization (correct)

C. Binding Corporate Rules

D. keeping all data in the country of origin

Explanation: very important to know as a privacy professional, the EU laws are something to look into (as will the laws in other countries that follow be). In the US there are still restrictions on processing data on citizens of the European Union, regardless of country of ownership, so B is the correct answer.

18. Which of the following is true about privacy notices?

A. only certain US laws require a privacy notice (correct)

B. privacy notices are required for all websites in the US or targeted at a US audience

C. changing a privacy notice mid-service is not deceptive

D. the CLOUD Act

Explanation: A is the correct answer. C is false and B is partly true depending on the type of website. D is just a name and does not answer the question.

19. What does workforce training on privacy matters establish?

A. it eliminates all compliance risk

B. the training motivates the workforce, and allows the workforce to work more efficiently

C. it shows that management delegates the process of becoming compliant

D. increase the level of knowledge of staff, decreasing the chance of non-compliance (correct)

Explanation: the key to effective training is to make clear what is expected and in doing so reduce non-compliance risk, so D is the correct answer. A may seem correct, but you can never eliminate all compliance risk.

20. A merger between a US based company, and affiliates in Asia and Canada is planned to take place. As a privacy officer, what considerations would you bring to the CEO's attention?

A. Canada's non-Personal Information Protection and Electronic Documents Act legislation

B. the potential benefits of sharing data

C. an expansion of your department and an increase in salary

D. data flow mapping (correct)

Explanation: data flow mapping is a great way to see which data you have and where they are going and coming from, so a great way to see which requirements you have to comply with for which data. D is the correct answer, A is less complete, B is not the responsibility of a privacy officer and C is less important.

21. What is one of the important considerations for companies selling to consumers internationally?

A. the salary of the privacy officers

B. whether they actively target customers in other countries (correct)

C. Bring Your Own Device practices

D. the Fourth amendment

Explanation: when targeting different countries, different legislation could apply, which needs to be checked. B is the correct answer.

22. What is the name of the guidelines developed by the Asia-Pacific Economic Cooperation?

A. the OECD guidelines

B. the IT Act

C. the Fair Information Practices

D. the APEC privacy framework (correct)

Explanation: just a fact, D is the correct answer. If you are not sure, the Fair Information Practices are usually your best bet if you do not know the answer (although not always the right answer).

23. Which of the following is not a key attribute of security?

A. Confidentiality

B. Delivery (correct)

C. Integrity

D. Availability

Explanation: the abbreviation to remember is CIA. Confidentiality, Integrity and Availability of the data. B is not part of CIA.

24. Which types of security controls can be considered in developing a security strategy?

A. physical, administrative, technical (correct)

B. proactive, reactive, distortive

C. detective, cumulative reactive

D. physical, cosmetic, digital

Explanation: in the context of security the controls are most often physical, administrative and technical. In other contexts, they can be different, but for your privacy exam A is the correct answer.

25. What is the best fitting description of a data breach?

A. a failure of security measures, resulting in the unauthorized accessing of data (correct)

B. loss of data, including an encrypted hard drive

C. a shutdown of the company server

D. the National Security Agency has access to classified information

Explanation: for a data breach, just remember that something must have gone wrong either malicious or by accident, where something did not work the way it should have worked (with exceptions depending on the definitions in the specific legislation). For now, A is the correct answer. B may seem correct, but it does not specify whether the data is accessed by someone or whether there is a backup.

26. After a data breach, there are several ways to deal with the breach. Which of the following is the least likely reason for correctly dealing with incidents?

A. to comply with legislation

B. to minimize adverse consequences

C. to hide security flaws (correct)

D. to fix any security weaknesses

Explanation: A, B and D are benefits of dealing with incidents correctly. C is deceptive and wrong, so the correct answer.

27. What is the biggest reason online privacy is a complicated thing?

A. smart devices automatically gather data

B. the Internet of Things is not controllable

C. people are social media addicts, and unable to stop sharing personal information

D. it is decentralized, non-transparent with a large collection of (seemingly) restrictive and contradicting legislation (correct)

Explanation: this is a vague question, similar to what you will encounter on the actual exam. Think about what the author of the question is looking for. Here, A and B are not correct as there is the possibility of human intervention, and C is assuming too much. So, D is the correct answer.

28. When a consent decree is published, what has happened?

A. a lawsuit is started regarding a data breach, resulting in a publication of the appropriate security policy

B. the Federal Trade Commission and the other party entered into an agreement to stop a certain conduct, and the information is published for other organizations to learn from (correct)

C. compensation is paid to the victims, so they cannot start a lawsuit

D. Binding Corporate Rules are implemented, ensuring consistent practices across all affiliates

Explanation: option B is correct, the others are false. When a consent decree is entered into, a party agrees to stop with an alleged illegal activity and the consent decree can help other organizations interpret rules and regulations.

29. How can the Federal Trade Commission be described best?

A. a part of the executive branch with rule-making powers (correct)

B. a counterpart of the European Parliament

C. the enforcer of the Fourth amendment

D. the Federal Trade Commission has won every case

Explanation: B and C are nonsense. D is false, the FTC did not win every case. A is the correct answer since it has some rule-making powers.

Use this scenario for the following two questions:

A well-known social media website called *Selfie Shenanigans* is constantly innovating. Innovating, of course, means finding ways to make a product out of its users. Users are incredibly happy with all services the website provides, and the website is working hard to keep figuring out new functionalities that users did not yet know they need.

In the next month, Selfie Shenanigans is planning to implement its newest feature in the US, only for its US users. The new feature allows Selfie Shenanigans to analyze all uploaded photos for visible signs of health issues, thus potentially algorithmically making life saving medical diagnoses.

Building a website is not cheap, and the CEO has so little money that he is basically an altruistic volunteer, so the data are sold to the user's health insurance company so it can inform the user of his or her medical diagnosis, if the health insurance company's records show that the user has not already received the required treatment.

You have been hired as a legal consultant, with the message that "the feature is getting implemented no matter what, but we just need you to tell us how to prevent trouble". The message is clear, and how you feel morally is not of importance.

30. Which law would least possibly be broken?

A. the Health Insurance Portability and Accountability Act

B. the Children's Online Privacy Protection Act

C. the General Data Protection Regulation (correct)

D. the Health Information Technology for Economic and Clinical Health Act

Explanation: option C applies only in the European Union, or when data subjects from the European Union are involved, hence is out of scope here. Remember this, because it might be instinctive to skip the question of whether a law applies given the way the question is phrased.

31. You find out that the website has a privacy notice that is shown before users sign up. What needs to happen?

A. the privacy notice needs to be changed, ensuring that the new feature can be implemented

B. a check whether the new practice is allowed for, according to the privacy notice, needs to be performed (correct)

C. all children under 13 years of age need to sign a new privacy notice

D. nothing, there is a privacy notice already, so it is fine, no need to worry

Explanation: it is a long shot, but perhaps the privacy notice that was agreed to covers the new practice. A may seem correct when reading quickly, but it implies retroactively changing a privacy notice, which means drastically changing an agreement one-sidedly and is likely not allowed here.

32. When does the Children's Online Privacy Protection Act apply?

A. for websites targeting children under 18

B. for websites targeting children under 13 (correct)

C. for websites without a privacy notice

D. for websites that store de-identified data of toddlers

Explanation: B is the correct answer. That is when COPPA applies. A is the wrong age, C makes no sense and D is out of scope since the data are de-identified (assuming that they cannot be traced back to the actual toddlers).

33. For which law does the Federal Trade Commission have specific authority?

A. the General Data Protection Regulation

B. the Children's Online Privacy Protection Act (correct)

C. the APEC Privacy Framework

D. the Fair Information Practices

Explanation: B is the only US law, so the answer is easy. Note that the Fair Information Practices are mentioned, which normally is your best chance of getting the question correct if you do not know the answer, but not in this case.

34. There are several laws concerning medical privacy, both on national and state level. Which of the following is the most likely reason for this legislation?

A. medical data are in high demand, hence legislation is needed to guide medical practitioners in the selling of such data

B. privacy is an absolute right, and therefore requires protection

C. organ theft is a major issue, and unsafely stored medical records were a valuable source of information for organ thieves

D. it is believed that patients are more open and honest about their conditions if they experience a sense of privacy (correct)

Explanation: you will probably find this in your study material, so D is the correct answer. Another reason is to make things go more efficiently, but that is not one of the options to choose from, resulting in D being the most likely answer.

35. What safeguard is often put in place by researchers when using medical data for research?

A. non-disclosure agreement

B. encryption of data

C. the data is de-identified (correct)

D. patient consent form

Explanation: de-identification lowers the risk of recognition. Option A, B, and D do not reduce the risk of the patient being recognized, so C is the most likely answer here as it offers the highest risk reduction. This is debatable, but you will find similar questions during the actual exam, so try to find a logical way of reasoning to the correct answer.

36. The Health Insurance Portability and Accountability Act is quite strict. Which of the following statements is most accurate?

A. all medical data are covered by the Health Insurance Portability and Accountability Act

B. the Health Insurance Portability and Accountability Act is based on the Fifth amendment

C. aspects of the Health Insurance Portability and Accountability Act can be disregarded when stricter state law is in place (correct)

D. all medical practitioners sign a Health Insurance Portability and Accountability Act declaration before being authorized to practice medicine

Explanation: HIPAA does not preempt stricter state law, so C is the correct answer. A is false, B is false, D is nonsense.

37. Which of the following best describes the privacy rights of a person visiting a doctor?

A. an absolute right, with full control over every aspect of the data, including control over the use for research

B. covered by the Health Insurance Portability and Accountability Act for the electronic transactions for the treatment, as well as the Reader Privacy Act for the book he bought in California to learn about the disease (correct)

C. the medical data derived from the visit to the doctor can under no circumstances be used for research

D. only the government is forbidden access to the data, based on the Fourth amendment, which includes e-health data generated by medical practitioners

Explanation: B is correct. The Reader Privacy Act was thrown in there to mislead the reader, but it is the correct answer. For A, C and D you have to remember that privacy is always balanced with other interests.

38. According to the Confidentiality of Substance Use Disorder Patient Record Rule, what is required for disclosure of patient information?

A. a recommendation from the patient's counselor

B. fully documented parental consent, regardless of the age of the patient

C. written patient consent, explicitly describing the type of information to be disclosed (correct)

D. under no circumstances is patient information to be disclosed

Explanation: this is only a small part of your study material probably, but details like this will be asked. The correct answer is C. A, B and D may have some seeming likeliness of being correct if unfamiliar with the details, but only C is correct.

39. What was the initial reason for the Health Insurance Portability and Accountability Act?

A. patient privacy and security

B. to define Personal Health Information

C. to define electronic Personal Health Information

D. the improvement of the efficiency of delivery of health care (correct)

Explanation: improving efficiency of the delivery of health care was one of the reasons. If there were clear rules for allowing electronic transfer of Personal Health Information, this would also speed up the health care itself.

40. What is one of the limitations of the Health Insurance Portability and Accountability Act?

A. the Health Information Technology for Economic and Clinical Health Act was needed to define electronic Personal Health Information

B. the Health Insurance Portability and Accountability Act is a guideline and not a law

C. the Health Insurance Portability and Accountability Act is not applicable to situations involving retired citizens

D. some doctors are not covered by the Health Insurance Portability and Accountability Act (correct)

Explanation: a doctor who accepts only cash is not covered by HIPAA, hence D is the correct answer. The other options are not true.

41. Which of the following is not a key privacy protection under the Health Insurance Portability and Accountability Act?

A. layered privacy notices (correct)

B. administrative, physical and technical safeguards

C. a privacy professional for covered entities

D. individuals are allowed to access and copy a designated record set

Explanation: layered privacy notices are not part of HIPAA, hence A is the correct answer.

42. Which of the following preempts state law in most areas?

A. the Fair and Accurate Credit Transactions Act (correct)

B. the Fair Credit Reporting Act

C. the Gramm-Leach-Bliley Act

D. the Financial Turmoil Reconciliation Assurance Act

Explanation: of this list, FACTA is the only one that preempts state law to some extent. Hence A is the correct answer. B and C are not applicable, and D is a nonsense name.

43. The Fair Credit Reporting Act affects organizations like Equifax, Experian and TransUnion. What are these organizations classified as?

A. Consumer Reporting Agencies (correct)

B. Credit Reporting Agencies

C. Credit Score Agencies

D. Transaction Recording Agencies

Explanation: they are Consumer Reporting Agencies, so A is the correct answer. The other answers are made up to sound similar, but are wrong.

44. Which of the following is required by the Fair and Accurate Credit Transactions Act and enhances privacy?

A. receipts are legally stored for a period of seven years

B. credit card numbers are only allowed to be stored without the accompanying signature

C. receipts are not allowed to reveal a full credit card number or debit card number (correct)

D. receipts are only allowed to be issued digitally in specific situations

Explanation: one of the requirements is that a credit card number cannot be shown fully on a receipt. This prevents risking identity theft if the receipt falls in the wrong hands. C is the correct answer.

45. How can the disposal rule be most accurately described?

A. making sure unauthorized recipients dispose of a consumer report after there is no legal basis for it anymore

B. when issued, the unnecessary information is disposed of before issuing a report

C. physical copies need to be scanned and disposed of, and digital storage needs to be encrypted

D. a way to ensure that a consumer report is disposed of properly after it is no longer needed or allowed to be used (correct)

Explanation: the effect of the disposal rule is that the risk of data falling in the wrong hands is minimized by disposing of the data as soon as possible. D is the correct answer. C keeps the data too long, B is almost correct and A already has data in the wrong hands.

46. Which of the following is not true regarding the Red Flag Rule?

A. originally required through the Fair and Accurate Credit Transactions Act

B. authorized the Federal Trade Commission & federal banking agencies

C. certain financial entities are required to develop an identity theft detection program

D. requires insurance against Identity Theft (correct)

Explanation: the Red Flag Rule is there to detect identity theft. Insurance does not detect identity theft. D is the correct answer. B does not directly refer to the rule, and is a little misleading, but is required under the Red Flag Rule and not the correct answer. Keep an eye out for these tricks during the exam.

47. What was U.S. Bancorp accused of?

A. not properly encrypting the credit card data of its customers

B. illegal data transfers to India, due to outsourcing

C. sharing detailed customer information with a telemarketing firm (correct)

D. storing data of minors without the required parental consent

Explanation: US Bancorp shared too much, hence C is the correct answer.

48. What kind of institutions fall within the scope of the Family Educational Rights and Privacy Act?

A. all educational institutions fall within the scope

B. educational institutions that receive federal funding (correct)

C. it applies to educational institutions with exchange students

D. privately funded educational institutions

Explanation: B is the correct answer. Practically this means most of the others as well, but not necessarily, hence B is the correct answer.

49. Which type of information is still allowed to be disclosed under the Family Educational Rights and Privacy Act?

A. Grade Point Average

B. directory information (correct)

C. home addresses of students

D. health insurance coverage

Explanation: directory information is allowed to be disclosed, so B is the correct answer. Whether the other three fall under directory information is perhaps debatable, but B is 100% correct and hence the answer to the question.

50. Which of the following best describes the US National Do Not Call Registry?

A. a program implemented by the Federal Communications Commission, where phone numbers of US residents can be registered to be placed in the registry

B. the requirement for citizens to actively indicate that they are open to receiving unsolicited phone calls

C. a program implemented by the Federal Trade Commission, where phone numbers can be registered to be placed in the registry (correct)

D. an initiative that was sparked by the concept of the Internet of Things

Explanation: C best describes it. A is only partially correct and meant to mislead, and the others are just wrong.

51. What is not true about the Do Not Call Registry?

A. sellers and telemarketers are required to update their call lists annually (correct)

B. only sellers, telemarketers, and service providers may access the registry

C. violations can lead to civil penalties

D. the Do Not Call Registry is implemented by the Federal Trade Commission

Explanation: the call list is required to be updated every 31 days, so not annually. Answer A is correct. It is important to know the exact periods for something. During the exam, questions like this can show up and such details allow you to eliminate wrong answers.

52. Which of the following is not true regarding consent to allow telemarketers and sellers to call a consumer?

A. must include a signature

B. consent requires a privacy notice (correct)

C. must be in writing

D. consent must be clear and conspicuous

Explanation: there is no requirement for a privacy notice. Option B is the correct answer.

53. What are robocalls?

A. phone calls established through the automated dialing of random numbers

B. phone calls augmented with Artificial Intelligence

C. communication established through the Internet of Things

D. prerecorded calls (correct)

Explanation: Robocalls are prerecorded calls, hence D is the correct answer. A is also usually the case, but the essence of a robocall is that it is prerecorded.

54. The goal of the Controlling the Assault of Non-Solicited Pornography And Marketing Act is best described as which of the following?

A. apply a paternalistic filtering of pornographic material so as to raise slipping moral standards

B. a way to respect individual rights and provide a way to indicate how desirable the communication is (correct)

C. eliminate phishing attacks, and reducing the financial burden it causes

D. allow parents to be in control over what messages their children receive

Explanation: B is the correct answer. A is farfetched, C is not going to happen thus unrealistic, and D is incorrect.

55. Which of the following can be said about the Cable Communications Policy Act?

A. video rental records cannot be disclosed freely

B. it has become redundant due to internet television

C. certain damages as a result of violations can be recovered because it provides for private right of action (correct)

D. there is no such law as the Cable Communications Policy Act

Explanation: the Cable Communications Act allows for private right of action, so C is the correct answer.

56. Which state was the first to include a Do Not Track requirement in its laws?

A. New York

B. California (correct)

C. Washington

D. North Carolina

Explanation: a useless fact to know, but B is the correct answer. Also, California is generally a decent guess in case you do not know the correct answer.

57. Due to the 2007 revisions to the Federal Rules of Civil Procedure, what is now required?

A. a non-disclosure requirement for members of the jury

B. names omitted in court cases

C. encryption of e-discovery data

D. redacting sensitive personal information (correct)

Explanation: D is correct, information that poses risks is required to be redacted.

58. Which of the following is not required for a subpoena according to the Federal Rule of Civil Procedure 45?

A. state the court from which it is issued

B. state the title of the action and its civil action number

C. take photographic evidence of the receipt of the subpoena (correct)

D. mention a person's right to challenge or modify the subpoena

Explanation: photographic evidence is not the only thing valid as evidence. A, B and D are explicitly required, hence C is the correct answer.

59. How can courts prohibit the disclosure of personal information used or generated in litigation?

A. the court can issue a protective order (correct)

B. the court can issue a restrictive order

C. the court can issue a redactive order

D. the court can issue a national security letter

Explanation: A is the correct answer. B and C are purposely close in order to mislead, and D is just using a phrase that sounds familiar from a different section.

60. What was the main concern when posting personal information used in bankruptcy cases online?

A. stalking

B. family feuds

C. identity theft (correct)

D. data breaches

Explanation: when certain sensitive information is known, identity theft is a risk, hence C is the correct answer. A and B may also be concerns, but not the main concern. D is just wrong, because when it is posted online (and is public) it cannot be a breach.

61. Which of the following is not one of the four key guidelines from the Sedona Conference?

A. professionals from several disciplines should provide input into the e-mail retention policy

B. e-mail retention policies should continually be developed

C. a Chief Information Security Officer in charge of e-discovery (correct)

D. industry standards should be taken into account

Explanation: expect a few questions going into this level of detail on things you may not have found important enough to study in detail. C is the correct answer.

62. What is the Communications Assistance to Law Enforcement Act also referred to?

A. the Pen Register

B. the Digital Telephony Bill (correct)

C. the Wire

D. Track and Trace

Explanation: a useless fact to know, but B is the correct answer. These are little facts that you should remember because there are likely one or more of these on the exam. If you know the purpose of the Act, you can also try to reason towards the correct answer.

63. In 2016 the FBI was quarrelling with Apple. What was the quarrel about?

A. new firmware slowing down phones

B. helping gain access to the data on a seized phone (correct)

C. the tablets in the Federal Bureau of Investigation's office could not fit the micro-SD required for the investigation

D. a cloud security breach exposing pictures of celebrities

Explanation: B is the correct answer. The others also happened (except for C), but B was in the news in 2016.

64. Which of the following is most accurate regarding workplace privacy?

A. workplace privacy is the same in every state

B. US privacy protection at the workplace is the strictest in the world

C. workers have a high level of influence in workplace practices

D. there is no law that covers privacy specifically (correct)

Explanation: D is the correct answer, as there are only laws that have an effect on workplace privacy but do not explicitly address it. State laws may vary, which is also why A is incorrect. B is not true and C is also not true (unless you consider quitting your job a high level of influence).

65. Which of the following is not a source of privacy protection for employees?

A. state labor laws

B. contract and tort law

C. overarching employment privacy law (correct)

D. certain federal laws

Explanation: there is no overarching employment privacy law in the US, hence C is the correct answer. The other options provide privacy protection to some extent for employees.

66. What is the most accurate comparison between US and EU workplace privacy?

A. the US inspired the EU legislation

B. the EU has no law that is applicable to the workplace

C. the US has cubicles, whereas in the EU cubicles are forbidden because of privacy concerns

D. EU employee data fall under the scope of the General Data Protection Regulation and offers more protection than all US laws combined (correct)

Explanation: A, B, and C are nonsense. D is the least incorrect answer. The General Data Protection Regulation is comprehensive and covers personal data at work as well. In the US, there are situations where workers enjoy little protection of their personal information.

67. What can be said about the Constitution's Fourth Amendment?

A. it provides protection from employers

B. it provides protection from government employers (correct)

C. it does not concern privacy

D. it only protects against the king of England

Explanation: B is the correct answer, as it applies to government searches.

68. In the US, there is employment at will. What is a consequence of this?

A. all legislation is rendered invalid

B. you can buy privacy

C. many aspects, covered by laws in other continents, are at the discretion of the employer (correct)

D. employees have no rights

Explanation: detrimental to workplace conditions, an employer can get away with a lot of things. C is the correct answer.

69. Which of the following is not a tort that can be relied on by an employee in a privacy case?

A. intrusion upon seclusion

B. publicity given to private life

C. defamation

D. intellectual property (correct)

Explanation: D has nothing to do with privacy, hence is the correct answer.

70. Of the following laws, which does not have employment privacy implications?

A. the Children's Online Privacy Protection Act (correct)

B. the Employee Retirement Income Security Act

C. the Health Insurance Portability and Accountability Act

D. the Fair Labor Standards Act

Explanation: unless you employ children under 13 years of age, A is the correct answer (you do not even have to know what the implications of the other options are).

71. At which state of employment do employers need to take into account workplace privacy considerations?

A. before employment

B. before, during, and after employment (correct)

C. during employment

D. after employment

Explanation: all phases of employment are impacted, so B is the correct answer since the others are incomplete. There may also be times during the exam where the answers are correct but incomplete. In that case, do not automatically dismiss it if the other answers are complete yet incorrect.

72. What is true about Bring Your Own Device policies?

A. only company-issued equipment is allowed to be used

B. it brings along security risks and requires reconsideration of the level of monitoring (correct)

C. employees surrender their data when a Bring Your Own Device policy is in place

D. Bring Your Own Device practices are illegal

Explanation: since employees bring their own devices, there may be restrictions on the extent to which you can monitor what they do with their devices, as it may expose sensitive information you are not allowed to see. As a privacy professional, try to stay away from BYOD practices. B is the correct answer.

73. Which of the following is a consequence of the Employee Polygraph Protection Act?

A. only grade A and B type polygraphs are allowed to be used

B. an employer cannot use a polygraph test to screen an applicant (correct)

C. a statement of sincerity is required to substitute a polygraph

D. employers cannot screen applicants

Explanation: B is correct. A and C are nonsense, and D is not true as there are more ways of screening than with a polygraph.

74. Which of the following agencies is not responsible for privacy enforcement?

A. the Federal Trade Commission

B. the Department of Education (correct)

C. the Federal Communications Commission

D. certain agencies part of the executive branch

Explanation: the Department of Education is the least likely to enforce privacy (although this does not mean that it never does). B is the answer that will be considered correct here.

75. What is true for the Federal Trade Commission?

A. the Federal Trade Commission is an independent agency (correct)

B. the Federal Trade Commission falls under direct control of the president

C. the Federal Trade Commission focuses solely on privacy

D. the Federal Trade Commission focuses solely on security

Explanation: B, C and D are false. A is the correct answer, as the Federal Trade Commission is an independent agency and does not fall under the direct control of the president.

76. What was the issue in the Designerware, LLC case?

A. the leaking of credit card numbers

B. key loggers, unexpected screenshots and photographs (correct)

C. a break-in on one of the servers that stored social security numbers

D. unauthorized disclosure of collected sensitive data

Explanation: expect a few case questions like this on the exam. B is the correct answer, as Designerware did some creepy things with the hardware they provided.

77. When is a data breach required to be reported?

A. above 200 persons

B. above 100 persons

C. if minors are involved

D. depends on the state and breach size (correct)

Explanation: breach reporting requirements can differ per state and field, so D is the most correct answer.

78. Is ransomware a data breach?

A. always

B. never

C. depends on whether unauthorized access has been established (correct)

D. not if the information was backed up

Explanation: if the ransomware also transmits the data (for example), it can also be considered a breach. A and B are too extreme, and D is not relevant. C is the correct answer.

Use this scenario for the following four questions:

A US-based supermarket chain called *Vallmart* performed poorly the last few months, due to a scandal which involved one of its employees dying because of exhaustion after a 20-hour shift. Vallmart executives tried to restore the store's reputation by offering all employees free in-house medical checkups. To keep things fair for those employees who already underwent a medical checkup at their regular doctor, Vallmart will reimburse any checkups already performed (up to a certain amount, of course).

As a second move to improve revenue, an aggressive takeover of the French Parrefour has taken place. Parrefour has an excellent customer loyalty program, which Vallmart is planning to merge with its own customer loyalty program. Doing so will allow Vallmart to predict global trends based on the data collected through the loyalty cards.

You are the Chief Privacy Officer of Vallmart, in charge of both the privacy officers of Vallmart and the privacy officers of the recently acquired Parrefour. Although you are not trained in European privacy law, you are aware of the potential existence of differences.

79. From an organizational perspective, what is likely the most prudent course of action?

A. place the US team in charge of the US data

B. request the US-based and EU-based privacy officers to educate each other on the applicable laws in their continent (correct)

C. place the EU team in charge of the EU data

D. fire the EU team and train the US team on EU law

Explanation: although perhaps also not realistic, B is the only option that addresses the problem of unfamiliarity with the laws and allows for cooperation. A and C are incomplete and D will waste too much time.

80. What is the most likely scenario for the use of the EU customer data?

A. the company is under full US ownership, so the data can be used freely

B. the data of the EU customers are deleted

C. the data cannot be used until the required safeguards are put in place (correct)

D. All EU customers receive a notice and a one-off discount on their shopping, agreeing their data are used in the US

Explanation: there are restrictions to what you can do with EU customer data. This includes the level of security and the compatibility with the privacy notice (a.o.). C is the correct option, D is invalid consent, B is unlikely as it can also be irreversibly de-identified and still be useful, and A is false.

81. Now that the US-based Vallmart has complete ownership of Parrefour, which of the following is most likely true?

A. US data are forbidden to be processed in Europe

B. the Federal Trade Commission and the Federal Communications Commission are the regulatory authorities that Vallmart has to answer to (correct)

C. US customers are granted the same rights in the US as Europeans had in Europe

D. medical information of US employees is free to be stored in Europe without additional safeguards

Explanation: A, C and D are perhaps possible, but unlikely, hence the factually correct B is the answer here.

82. Which of the following is most probable regarding workplace monitoring at Vallmart (including Parrefour)?

A. the company is US owned now, so either accept it or find a new job (employment at will)

B. the US practices may have to be revised (correct)

C. a salary increase for EU employees will be negotiated with the labor unions to compensate for the loss of privacy

D. Europe is full of socialists, so the workers will not mind sacrificing privacy for the greater good (the company)

Explanation: since there is a big difference between the powers of employers in the US and in the European Union, perhaps not everything can be implemented in the newly acquired supermarket. B is the correct answer. D and C are nonsense, and A is false.

83. Certain national laws preempt state law. Out of the following choices, how can preempting best be described?

A. a privacy notice, under many circumstances, can be overruled by state law

B. laws of an inferior government can be superseded by those of a superior government (correct)

C. if a state has no law, it is preempted by national law

D. federal judges can preempt the president and a large part of the executive branch

Explanation: B is correct and answers the question. A does not address the question, and C and D are incorrect.

84. Although there are many actions an individual can take to battle injustice, which of the following most accurately describes private right of action?

A. to carry a concealed weapon and use it to protect your privacy when someone attempts to enter your domicile

B. to start a lawsuit when a law is violated (correct)

C. to enforce the binding rules of a privacy notice

D. to forbid organizations from processing the data of minors that you are the legal guardian of

Explanation: B is correct, the others are somewhat farfetched.

85. If an agency has authority, there are two types of authority that agency can have. Which type of authority does the Federal Trade Commission have?

A. general authority

B. specific authority

C. general authority as well as specific authority (correct)

D. operational authority

Explanation: C is correct, the Federal Trade Commission has both types of authority. D is nonsense and A and B are incomplete.

86. Many references to privacy can be found all throughout recorded history. When looking at laws regarding personal information, which class of privacy does law concerning personal information pertain to?

A. bodily privacy

B. territorial privacy

C. communications privacy

D. information privacy (correct)

Explanation: D is correct, the information is in the name personal *information*. It is also in the name Fair *Information* Privacy Practices.

87. Which of the following is not (yet) part of the Fair Information Practices?

A. notice

B. choice and consent

C. disclosure

D. legal basis (correct)

Explanation: study the Fair Information Practices. They will show up on the exam. D is not a Fair Information Practice.

88. All over the world, different models of privacy protection are adopted. Which of the following is true regarding models of privacy protection?

A. in the US there is a sectoral model, and in the EU there is a comprehensive model (correct)

B. the US only uses the co-regulatory model

C. Europe has a strong focus on the self-regulatory model

D. the laws in the US fall under the comprehensive model

Explanation: A is the correct answer, the others are false. Remember that in the US there are no comprehensive federal privacy laws (yet).

89. Which of the following best describes the relationship between case law and common law?

A. common law needs case law to exist (correct)

B. common law is based on principles

C. case law is solely the judge's opinion

D. case law is fluid, and allows for presidential intervention

Explanation: option A is the only one that addresses the question. The legal principles of common law have developed in case law.

90. When can an organization most likely be in trouble for violating contract law?

A. when someone provided his or her data based on the practices mentioned in the privacy notice (correct)

B. when a data subject disagrees with a privacy notice

C. when a privacy notice is not in the local language

D. when a privacy notice is not on the organization's website

Explanation: option A is correct, as in this instance the privacy notice can be seen as a contract.

Made in the USA
Coppell, TX
26 January 2021

48849286R00046